Pray Deep
IGNITE YOUR *prayer life*

40-Day Prayer Journal

Copyright ©2021 Kathryn P. Shirey
Published by San Marco Publications
Frisco, TX

All Scripture quotations, unless otherwise indicated, are taken from the Holy Bible, New International Version®, NIV®. Copyright ©1973, 1978, 1984, 2011 by Biblica, Inc.™ Used by permission of Zondervan. All rights reserved worldwide. www.zondervan.com The "NIV" and "New International Version" are trademarks registered in the United States Patent and Trademark Office by Biblica, Inc.™

All Rights Reserved.
No part of this book may be reproduced or transmitted in any form or by any means including but not limited to information storage and retrieval systems, electronic, mechanical, photocopy, recording, etc. without written permission from the copyright holder.

ISBN: 978-1-7344819-3-8

First printing, October 2021

Using the Pray Deep
Prayer Journal

This prayer journal is designed to accompany the Pray Deep course.

While these prayers are included within each lesson in the course workbook, this journal pulls them all out into a combined 40-day prayer guide.

Instructions for using each prayer method referenced are included in the Pray Deep course workbook.

I encourage you to try new ways to pray, explore each of the methods and prayers suggested here. Dive into the conversations prompted, examine your feelings about prayer with God, and allow him to begin working in your heart in new ways.

Praying for you,
~Kathryn

Day 1: The *Discipline* of Prayer

Open the conversation with God.

Share your day with God, give him praise and thanks, share your concerns, and ask for his guidance.

Tip: You can find a guide to Prayer as a Conversation on page 22 of the Pray Deep course workbook.

Day 2: The *Discipline* of Prayer

Pray the Lord's Prayer slowly.

Say each line, pausing to consider each of the words. It may help to read the words as you pray. Focus on each word, each phrase, praying about what it means in your life today.

Tip: You can find the Lord's Prayer in your Bible in Matthew 6:9-13 or Luke 11:2-4.

Day 3: The *Discipline* of Prayer

Respond to the Lord's Prayer.

Pray the Lord's Prayer, responding to each line in the prayer. After each phrase, stop and respond to God.

Tip: You can find a guide to Praying the Lord's Prayer on page 24 of the Pray Deep course workbook.

Day 4: The *Discipline* of Prayer

Pray your own version of the Lord's Prayer.

Write your own prayer based on the Lord's Prayer. Pray each section in your own words, going as deep as you want.

Tip: You can find an outline of the Lord's Prayer on page 24 of the Pray Deep course workbook.

Day 5: The *Discipline* of Prayer

Pray the ACTS Prayer.

Pray using the ACTS method. Take time to pray through each of the sections—Adoration, Confession, Thanksgiving, and Supplication.

Tip: You can find a guide to the ACTS Prayer on page 29 of the Pray Deep course workbook.

Day 6: The *Conversation* of Prayer

Pray through a topic you don't cover often in your prayers.

Focus on one prayer topic today. Go deep with God discussing that topic. You can simply talk to God in prayer or use a prayer journal to write out your thoughts and prayers.

Tip: You can find a list of prayer conversation topics on page 33 of the Pray Deep course workbook.

Day 7: The *Conversation* of Prayer

Pray through Scripture or prayer journaling.

Choose a form of praying with Scripture or prayer journaling you haven't used before or don't use often. Use that for your prayers today.

Tip: You can find guides in the Pray Deep course workbook for praying with Scripture (page 85), praying with Psalms (page 88), Lectio Divina (page 109), Gospel contemplation (page 56), and prayer journaling (page 73).

Day 8: The *Conversation* of Prayer

Pray through art or music.

Choose a form of praying with art or music you haven't used before or don't use often. Use that for your prayers today.

Tip: You can find guides in the Pray Deep course workbook for praying with prayer doodles (page 122), Visio Divina (page 153), and praying with music (page 53).

Day 9: The *Conversation* of Prayer

Pray a listening prayer.

Choose a form of listening prayer you haven't used before or don't use often. Use that for your prayers today.

Tip: You can find guides in the Pray Deep course workbook for listening prayer (page 107), Lectio Divina (page 109), and Examen (page 91).

Day 10: The *Conversation* of Prayer

Pray with a prayer posture you don't often use.

Choose a different prayer posture for your prayers today than what you typically use. Observe how the posture of your body affects your prayers and the posture of your heart.

Tip: You can find a list of different postures for prayer on page 37 of the Pray Deep course workbook.

Day 11: The *Challenges* of Prayer

Pray with a worship song.

Try praying with music today. Find a worship song you like or that's been speaking to your heart. Play it and sing along, using the song as your prayer.

Tip: You can find a guide to praying with music on page 53 of the Pray Deep course workbook.

Day 12: The *Challenges* of Prayer

Pray with a written prayer.

Start your prayer time with a written prayer. Choose a prayer from the Book of Common Prayer, one from our newsletters, or from any book of prayers. Use this prayer to get your words started, adding in your own details as you pray.

Tip: You can find a guide to praying with written prayers on page 51 of the Pray Deep course workbook.

Day 13: The *Challenges* of Prayer

Try a new form of prayer today.

Try something new today. Choose a prayer method that interests you or that you haven't tried yet.

Tip: The Pray Deep course workbook includes guides to 22 different ways to pray. Look at the table of contents to find a prayer method you want to try.

Day 14: The *Challenges* of Prayer

Journal your prayer today.

Write out a prayer to God, sharing where you struggle with prayer. Talk about what you're learning through the difficulties and ask God for help to work through it.

Tip: You can find a guide to prayer journaling on page 73 of the Pray Deep course workbook.

Day 15: The *Challenges* of Prayer

Pray in a new location today.

Pray in a different location from where you typically pray. Take your prayers outside or to a different spot than you normally pray. Note how the change of location affects your prayers and your focus.

Day 16: The *Disappointment* of Prayer

Pray for your prayers to be answered in God's time.

Pray through what "in God's time" means and how you can accept God's timetable as you wait for him to answer your prayers.

Day 17: The *Disappointment* of Prayer

Pray for your prayers to be answered in God's way.

Explore what it means for your prayers to be answered in God's way, not yours. How do you need to release your expectations and plans so that God can answer your prayers in his way?

Day 18: The *Disappointment* of Prayer

Pray for your prayers to be answered to God's will.

Pray for your prayers to be answered to God's will, not yours. How can you submit to God's will over your life and the prayer requests you're praying? What does that look like?

Day 19: The *Disappointment* of Prayer

Pray for your prayers to be answered to God's glory.

How might God be bringing glory to himself and his kingdom through his answer to your prayers? Pray that whatever answer he provides will help grow his kingdom.

Day 20: The *Disappointment* of Prayer

Pray over your unanswered prayers.

Go deep with God today, exploring how he might already be answering, what work you need to do to align your will with his, or how you need to prepare your heart for what's next. Pray for him to answer your prayers in his time, in his way, and always to his glory.

Day 21: The *Relationship* of Prayer

Pray through Mark 2:13-17.

Once again Jesus went out beside the lake. A large crowd came to him, and he began to teach them. As he walked along, he saw Levi son of Alphaeus sitting at the tax collector's booth. "Follow me," Jesus told him, and Levi got up and followed him.

While Jesus was having dinner at Levi's house, many tax collectors and sinners were eating with him and his disciples, for there were many who followed him. When the teachers of the law who were Pharisees saw him eating with the sinners and tax collectors, they asked his disciples: "Why does he eat with tax collectors and sinners?"

On hearing this, Jesus said to them, "It is not the healthy who need a doctor, but the sick. I have not come to call the righteous, but sinners."

(Mark 2:13-17 NIV)

Tip: Try praying Gospel Contemplation with this passage. You can find a guide for this on page 56 of the Pray Deep course workbook.

Day 22: The *Relationship* of Prayer

Pray through John 10:1-18.

"I am the good shepherd; I know my sheep and my sheep know me— just as the Father knows me and I know the Father—and I lay down my life for the sheep. I have other sheep that are not of this sheep pen. I must bring them also. They too will listen to my voice, and there shall be one flock and one shepherd. The reason my Father loves me is that I lay down my life—only to take it up again. No one takes it from me, but I lay it down of my own accord. I have authority to lay it down and authority to take it up again. This command I received from my Father."

(John 10:14-18 NIV)

Tip: You can find a guide to praying through Scripture on page 85 of the Pray Deep course workbook.

Day 23: The *Relationship* of Prayer

Pray through Psalm 16.

Lord, you alone are my portion and my cup;
you make my lot secure.
The boundary lines have fallen for me in pleasant places;
surely I have a delightful inheritance.
I will praise the Lord, who counsels me;
even at night my heart instructs me.
I keep my eyes always on the Lord.
With him at my right hand, I will not be shaken.

Therefore my heart is glad and my tongue rejoices;
my body also will rest secure,
because you will not abandon me to the realm of the dead,
nor will you let your faithful one see decay.
You make known to me the path of life;
you will fill me with joy in your presence,
with eternal pleasures at your right hand.

(Psalm 16:5–11 NIV)

Tip: You can find a guide to praying through Psalms on page 88 of the Pray Deep course workbook.

Day 24: The *Relationship* of Prayer

Pray through Psalm 25.

Show me your ways, Lord,
teach me your paths.

Guide me in your truth and teach me,
for you are God my Savior,
and my hope is in you all day long.

Remember, Lord, your great mercy and love,
for they are from of old.

Do not remember the sins of my youth
and my rebellious ways;

according to your love remember me,
for you, Lord, are good.

(Psalm 25:4-7 NIV)

Tip: Try praying with Lectio Divina today. You can find a guide for this on page 109 of the Pray Deep course workbook.

Day 25: The *Relationship* of Prayer

Pray the Examen.

Review your day with Jesus using the Examen prayer. What did you do well today? Where do you have room for improvement? Ask him to help you do better tomorrow.

Tip: You can find a guide to praying the Examen on page 91 of the Pray Deep course workbook.

Day 26: The *Power* of Prayer

Pray a listening prayer.

Sit in the silence with God today. Set a timer for five minutes and pray a silent, listening prayer. Be attentive to hear God's voice in your heart.

Tip: You can find a guide to listening prayer on page 107 of the Pray Deep course workbook.

Day 27: The *Power* of Prayer

Pray through Lectio Divina using Mark 1:14-20

As Jesus walked beside the Sea of Galilee, he saw Simon and his brother Andrew casting a net into the lake, for they were fishermen. "Come, follow me," Jesus said, "and I will send you out to fish for people." At once they left their nets and followed him.

When he had gone a little farther, he saw James son of Zebedee and his brother John in a boat, preparing their nets. Without delay he called them, and they left their father Zebedee in the boat with the hired men and followed him.

(Mark 1:16-20 NIV)

Tip: You can find a guide to Lectio Divina on page 109 of the Pray Deep course workbook.

Day 28: The *Power* of Prayer

Pray "make me", instead of "give me."

Try this one-word shift in your prayers today. Instead of "give me", pray "make me".

"Father, make me into who you want me to be."

Pray this until you feel a shift in your heart and sense the door opening to a more personal relationship with God.

Day 29: The *Power* of Prayer

Pray a longer listening prayer today.

Spend a longer time in silence with God today. Set a timer for 15 minutes. Prepare your heart, ask God to enter into the conversation and speak to you, and then just sit silently in his presence and listen.

Tip: You can find a guide to praying a listening prayer on page 107 of the Pray Deep course workbook.

Day 30: The *Power* of Prayer

Pray through Lectio Divina using Acts 4:23-31.

Now, Lord, consider their threats and enable your servants to speak your word with great boldness. Stretch out your hand to heal and perform signs and wonders through the name of your holy servant Jesus."

After they prayed, the place where they were meeting was shaken. And they were all filled with the Holy Spirit and spoke the word of God boldly.

(Acts 4:29-31 NIV)

Tip: You can find a guide to praying Lectio Divina on page 109 of the Pray Deep course workbook.

Day 31: The *Battlefield* of Prayer

Pray to invite God into your battles.

Share the current trials you're facing with God. Ask him to walk beside, lead, and fight for you through the hard times. Work to hand over control of the battle to him.

Day 32: The *Battlefield* of Prayer

Praise God through your trials.

Spend time today simply praising God for who he is, not just what he's done. Sing his praises and focus on his goodness.

Day 33: The *Battlefield* of Prayer

Pray over your prayer list using prayer doodles.

Today, try using prayer doodles to take your time praying for others. Take your prayer list and pray over it by doodling around each name, lingering, and lifting each person and their needs up to God.

Tip: You can find a guide for praying with prayer doodles on page 122 of the Pray Deep course workbook.

Day 34: The *Battlefield* of Prayer

Take a physical or virtual prayer walk today.

Take a prayer walk—physical or virtual. Decide what kind of prayer walk you'll do and then take your prayers to the street.

Tip: You can find instructions for prayer walking on page 125 of the Pray Deep course workbook. You can also find ideas for virtual prayer walks on page 128.

Day 35: The *Battlefield* of Prayer

Pray the prayer of King Jehoshaphat.

Pray your own version of the prayer King Jehoshaphat prayed in 2 Chronicles 20. Release your concerns to God. Trust that he has a plan and is fighting for you.

Tip: You can find a guide for praying the prayer of King Jehoshaphat on page 130 of the Pray Deep course workbook.

Day 36: The *Journey* of Prayer

Pray the five finger prayer.

Pray for others today, using the five finger prayer. Use this prayer to think of all those who need your prayers today.

Tip: You can find a guide to praying the five finger prayer on page 140 of the Pray Deep course workbook.

Day 37: The *Journey* of Prayer

Choose a prompt and pray throughout the day.

Choose something you see throughout your day and decide on a prayer you'll say when you see it. Then, throughout the day today, say a quick prayer each time you see your prompt.

Tip: You can find a guide for praying with every day prayer prompts on page 142 of the Pray Deep course workbook.

Day 38: The *Journey* of Prayer

Pray with Anglican prayer beads.

Try praying with prayer beads today. If you don't have prayer beads, use a sample prayer and follow along as if you had beads in your hands.

Tip: You can find a guide and sample prayer for praying with Anglican prayer beads on page 149 of the Pray Deep course workbook.

Day 39: The *Journey* of Prayer

Pray through Visio Divina.

Choose an image (a piece of art, a photo, a scene from nature) and use it to pray through Visio Divina.

Tip: You can find a guide for praying through Visio Divina on page 153 of the Pray Deep course workbook.

Day 40: The *Journey* of Prayer

Pray to continue learning and growing on the journey of prayer.

Ask God to continue teaching you and helping you grow in your faith. Commit to keep learning as you progress along the journey of prayer.

Meet Kathryn

Kathryn Shirey is an ordinary girl following an extraordinary God, writing about prayer, trusting God, growing faith, and stepping into all of God's possibilities for your life at PrayerandPossibilities.com.

A recovering prayer skeptic who's experienced first-hand the power of prayer, she's passionate about guiding others to discover the transformation possible through prayer.

Find other devotionals and prayer resources at: shop.PrayerandPossibilities.com

Connect with Kathryn:

Blog: www.PrayerandPossibilities.com

Facebook: www.facebook.com/PrayerandPossibilities

Pinterest: www.pinterest.com/kpshirey

Twitter: www.twitter.com/KathrynPShirey

Instagram: www.instagram.com/prayer.and.possibilities/

Prayer + possibilities
WITH KATHRYN SHIREY

Made in the USA
Middletown, DE
09 October 2021